Great Americans
George Washington Carver

Barbara Kiely Miller

Reading consultant: Susan Nations, M.Ed., author/literacy coach/
consultant in literacy development

WEEKLY READER®
PUBLISHING

Please visit our web site at: **www.garethstevens.com**
For a free color catalog describing our list of high-quality books,
call 1-800-542-2595 (USA) or 1-800-387-3178 (Canada).

Library of Congress Cataloging-in-Publication Data

Kiely Miller, Barbara.
   George Washington Carver / by Barbara Kiely Miller.
     p. cm. — (Great Americans)
   Includes bibliographical references and index.
   ISBN-13: 978-0-8368-8313-8 (lib. bdg.)
   ISBN-13: 978-0-8368-8320-6 (softcover)
   ISBN-10: 0-8368-8313-6 (lib. bdg.)
   ISBN-10: 0-8368-8320-9 (softcover)
   1. Carver, George Washington, 1864-1943—Juvenile literature. 2. African American
agriculturists—Biography—Juvenile literature. 3. Agriculturists—United States—Biography—
Juvenile literature. I. Title.
   S417.C3K54 2007
   630.92—dc22
                              2007011279

This edition first published in 2008 by
Weekly Reader® Books
An imprint of Gareth Stevens Publishing
1 Reader's Digest Road
Pleasantville, NY 10570-7000 USA

Copyright © 2008 by Gareth Stevens, Inc.

Managing editor: Valerie J. Weber
Art direction: Tammy West
Cover design and page layout: Charlie Dahl
Picture research: Sabrina Crewe
Production: Jessica Yanke

Picture credits: Cover, title page, p. 5 © Getty Images; pp. 6, 7 George Washington
Carver National Monument; p. 9 Used by permission, State Historical Society of
Missouri, Columbia; p. 10 Iowa State University Library Special Collections Department;
p. 11 Charlie Dahl/© Gareth Stevens, Inc.; p. 13 (both) U.S. Department of Agriculture;
p. 14 © Bettmann/Corbis; pp. 15, 16 Library of Congress; p. 17 National Archives and
Records Administration; p. 18 Courtesy National Park Service Museum Management
Program and Tuskegee Institute National Historic Site; p. 20 Tuskegee Institute National
Historic Site; p. 21 © Jeff Greenberg/PhotoEdit.

Printed in the United States of America

1 2 3 4 5 6 7 8 9 11 10 09 08 07

Table of Contents

Chapter 1: A Young Scientist 4

Chapter 2: Becoming a Teacher 8

Chapter 3: Helping Farmers and Students . . . 12

Chapter 4: Scientist for the World 19

Glossary 22

For More Information 23

Index 24

Cover and title page: George Washington Carver was a scientist. His work with plants, soil, and fertilizers helped farmers around the world.

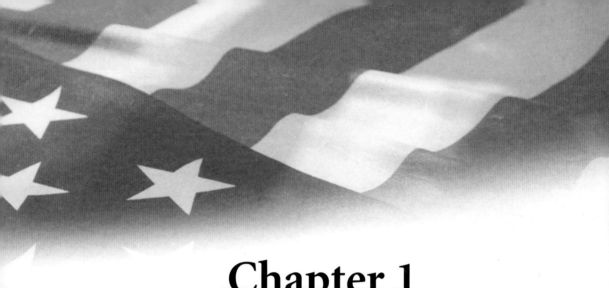

Chapter 1

A Young Scientist

George Washington Carver was at work in his **lab**.
His table held glass bottles, a scale, and other tools.
He also had a pile of peanuts. Carver was making
new foods and products out of them. Can you
imagine turning peanuts into plastics and paper?
Carver could — and did!

Carver made more than three hundred products out of peanuts, from shampoo to gas! He invented many other things using sweet potatoes. Carver also taught farmers how to keep their soil healthy and grow better **crops**. George Washington Carver is the world's most famous African American scientist.

Taken in 1935, this photo shows Carver at age seventy working in his lab.

Built in 1881, Moses Carver's farmhouse still stands in Missouri. It replaced the cabin that George grew up in.

George Washington Carver was born in 1864 near Diamond Grove, Missouri. His parents were slaves. Soon after George was born, his father died.

His mother worked on a farm owned by Moses Carver. When George was a baby, he and his mother were kidnapped. Carver traded a racehorse to get George back. George never saw his mother again, however.

Moses Carver and his wife raised George and his brother James. As a child, George was often sick and could not work. Instead, he liked walking through the woods, studying and gathering plants. George liked drawing flowers, too. He learned how to take care of plants so they would grow bigger and stronger. People called him the plant doctor.

This statue of a young George Washington Carver stands near Diamond Grove. It shows him holding a plant.

Chapter 2

Becoming a Teacher

During the late 1800s, black and white children went to separate schools. The closest school for black children was several miles from the Carvers' farm. George Washington Carver and his brother walked to school every day. George loved learning.

At age twelve, Carver left home to go to high school in Kansas. He worked on a farm to earn money for his food, clothes, and a place to sleep.

Carver loved to paint, but he dreamed of becoming a scientist. Many schools and businesses did not allow African Americans in then, however. Carver wanted to go to Iowa **Agricultural College**, but it would not let him in. Instead, he became the first black student at Simpson College in Indianola, Iowa. Three years later, the Iowa Agricultural College accepted him.

Carver's knowledge of plants shows in his paintings. One of his paintings won an award at the 1893 World's Fair in Chicago.

Carver studied the science of plants and farming. He graduated in 1894 and became the school's first black teacher. He continued his own studies, too. Carver became well known for his **experiments** with plants.

This is Carver's 1894 college graduation photo. Carver wrote several articles about plants and became known around the country.

Carver could have made lots of money working for a business. Instead, Carver agreed to teach at Tuskegee Institute in Chehaw, Alabama. Tuskegee is a college for black students.

This map shows the places in Kansas and Iowa where Carver went to school. Teaching at Tuskegee Institute took him even farther from his home in Diamond Grove.

Chapter 3

Helping Farmers and Students

At Tuskegee, Carver tested different plant seeds, soils, and **fertilizers**. The results of his experiments solved problems for farmers. His new fertilizers helped them raise more crops. He also grew new and better plants. Carver's work helped people become better farmers.

Farmers in southern states had grown cotton for one hundred years. Growing cotton every year removed **nutrients** from the soil, however. Carver discovered that growing peanuts, peas, or sweet potatoes put the nutrients back. He taught farmers that planting these crops every other year made the soil richer. Farmers were able to **harvest** more crops.

Farmers in the United States now grow about two hundred times as much peanuts (*left*) as they do cotton (*right*).

By experimenting, Carver learned he could use peanuts to make paper, ink, soap, rubber, dyes, and hundreds of other things.

Carver worked to find new uses for all these crops. He found hundreds of products could be made from peanuts and sweet potatoes, including shoe polish!

Farms that could not grow cotton could now raise other crops to be made into these products. Carver may have saved these farms from closing.

Carver made many paints and dyes from clay. He used the paint in his own art and let businesses use it, too. His paint helped poor farmers fix up their houses. Carver held onto his recipe for making paint and dyes from peanuts. He gave away all his other recipes and inventions.

As the head of the agricultural program at Tuskegee, Carver was able to share his discoveries with others for free and teach other young scientists.

Tuskegee Institute.
Tuskegee, Ala. April 5th 1915.

Carver lived and taught at Tuskegee for forty-seven years. This photo from 1902 shows him teaching a class in the laboratory.

Both in and out of the school, Carver was a great teacher. He did not give his students all the answers. Instead, he said they should run tests and figure out the answers themselves. Carver also spoke to people at schools, farms, and county fairs about better ways of farming.

To help teach people besides students, Carver invented a school that could be moved. This wagon pulled by horses brought farm experiments and ideas to people around town. Later, the school used a truck that carried teachers, a nurse, and others to talk with people in the countryside.

Tuskegee Institute was started by Booker T. Washington, an African American educator. The moveable school was named after him.

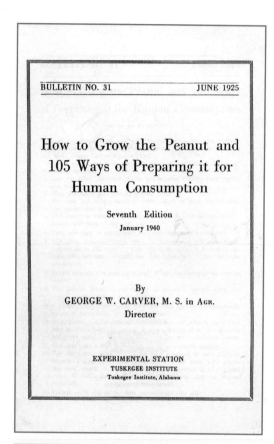

BULLETIN NO. 31   JUNE 1925

How to Grow the Peanut and
105 Ways of Preparing it for
Human Consumption

Seventh Edition
January 1940

By
GEORGE W. CARVER, M. S. in AGR.
Director

EXPERIMENTAL STATION
TUSKEGEE INSTITUTE
Tuskegee Institute, Alabama

One of Carver's booklets gave over one hundred ideas on how to cook peanuts for human consumption, or eating.

Carver wrote many booklets about growing and using crops. They included his recipes, such as peanut soup and peanut cookies.

In 1922, Carver spoke to members of Congress. He convinced the lawmakers to place a tax on peanuts from other countries. People would now buy more peanuts grown in the United States because they would cost less than other peanuts.

Chapter 4

Scientist for the World

George Washington Carver became well-known
throughout the world. Farmers in other countries asked
him for help with problems. He also became friends
with inventors such as Thomas Edison and carmaker
Henry Ford. In 1939, President Theodore Roosevelt
gave Carver an award for his work in science.

Carver never married. Although he could have taken a job that made him rich, he taught at Tuskegee his whole life. He saved his money and gave it all to the college so others could continue his work in the future.

Throughout his life, Carver looked at plants to see what they could teach him.

George Washington Carver died on January 5, 1943. Today, students can visit the Carver Science Discovery Center in Diamond, Missouri. There they can try some of Carver's experiments with soil, plants, and other materials. His work might have them dreaming of becoming scientists, too!

People can also visit the George Washington Carver Museum at the Tuskegee Institute. Photos and exhibits teach visitors about Carver's important discoveries and work.

Glossary

agricultural — describes something to do with farming

college — a school that many students go to after high school

Congress — the part of the U.S. government that makes laws

crops — plants that are grown and harvested for sale

experiments — tests done to discover something or to prove something

fertilizers — substances that are added to soil so plants will grow better

graduated — having finished classes or school and received a diploma

harvest — to gather a crop after it has grown

kidnapped — taken by force to another place by someone and usually kept to exchange for money

lab — short for laboratory, a room or building with special equipment that is used to do scientific experiments

nutrients — things that give plants and animals what they need to grow

recipe — a set of instructions for making something from different substances, usually food

slaves — people who are treated as property and are forced to work without pay. Slaves are not free.

For More Information

Books

George Washington Carver. Scholastic News Nonfiction Readers (series). Jo S. Kittinger (Children's Press)

George Washington Carver: The Peanut Scientist. Pat McKissack and Frederick McKissack (Enslow Publishers)

George Washington Carver: The Peanut Wizard. Smart About (series). Laura Driscoll (Grosset & Dunlap)

A Picture Book of George Washington Carver. Picture Book Biography (series). David A. Adler (Holiday House)

Web Sites

George Washington Carver Coloring and Activity Book
www.usda.gov/oo/colorbook.htm
Fun activities to help you learn more about peanuts and Carver.

National Peanut Board — Kid's Corner
www.nationalpeanutboard.org/kidscorner
Learn fun facts and make your own peanut butter.

Publisher's note to educators and parents: Our editors have carefully reviewed these Web sites to ensure that they are suitable for children. Many Web sites change frequently, however, and we cannot guarantee that a site's future contents will continue to meet our high standards of quality and educational value. Be advised that children should be closely supervised whenever they access the Internet.

Index

African Americans 5, 8, 9, 10, 11, 17

Carver, James 7, 8
Carver, Moses 6, 7,
Carver Science Discovery Center 21
colleges 9, 10
Congress 18
cotton 13, 14
crops 5, 12, 13, 14, 18

Edison, Thomas 19
experiments 10, 12, 14, 17, 21

families 6, 7
farmers/farming 5, 6, 8, 10, 12, 13, 14, 15, 16, 19
foods 4, 8
Ford, Henry 19

inventions 15

laboratories 4, 5, 16

painting 9
peanuts 4, 5, 13, 14, 15, 18
plants 7, 10, 12, 21
presidents 19
products 4, 14

recipes 15, 18

schools 8, 9, 10, 11, 16, 17
scientists 5, 9, 21
soils 5, 12, 13, 21
sweet potatoes 5, 13, 14

teaching 10, 11, 13, 15, 16
Tuskegee Institute 11, 12, 15, 16, 20, 21

About the Author

Barbara Kiely Miller is an editor and writer of educational books for children. She has a degree in creative writing from the University of Wisconsin–Milwaukee. Barbara lives in Shorewood, Wisconsin, with her husband and their two cats Ruby and Sophie. When she is not writing or reading books, Barbara enjoys photography, bicycling, and gardening.

HSCEX   +
           B
         C331K

KIELY MILLER, BARBARA
    GEORGE WASHINGTON
    CARVER
SCENIC WOODS
05/08